COOKING WITH BEER

Publications International, Ltd.

Microwave Cooking: Microwave ovens vary in wattage. Use the cooking times as guidelines and check for doneness before adding more time.

WARNING: Food preparartion, baking and cooking involve inherent dangers: misuse of electric products, sharp electric tools, boiling water, hot stoves, allergic reactions, foodborne illnesses and the like, pose numerous potential risks. Publications International, Ltd. (PIL) assumes no responsibility or liability for any damages you may experience as a result of following recipes, instructions, tips or advice in this publication.

While we hope this publication helps you find new ways to eat delicious foods, you many not always achieve the results desired due to variations in ingredients, cooking temperatures, typos, errors, omissions or individual cooking abilities.

Acknowledgments

The publisher would like to thank the companies and organizations listed below for the use of their recipes and photographs in this publication.

Campbell Soup Company
Cream of Wheat® Cereal,
   A Division of B&G Foods North America, Inc.
McCormick & Company, Inc.
© Sunbeam Products, Inc. doing business as
   Jarden Consumer Solutions.

Let's get social!

 @Publications_International

 @PublicationsInternational

www.pilbooks.com

TABLE
OF
CONTENTS

PARTY STARTERS

CHILI CHEESE FRIES

MAKES 4 SERVINGS

1½ pounds ground beef

1 medium onion, chopped

2 cloves garlic, minced

½ cup lager

2 tablespoons chili powder

2 tablespoons tomato paste

Salt and black pepper

1 package (32 ounces) frozen French fries

1 jar (15 ounces) cheese sauce, heated

Sour cream and chopped green onions (optional)

1 Brown beef, onion and garlic in large skillet over medium-high heat 6 to 8 minutes, stirring to break up meat. Drain fat.

2 Stir lager, chili powder and tomato paste into beef mixture. Simmer, stirring occasionally, 20 minutes or until most liquid has evaporated. Season with salt and pepper.

3 Meanwhile, bake French fries according to package directions.

4 Divide French fries evenly among bowls. Top evenly with chili and cheese sauce. Garnish with sour cream and green onions.

BEER-BATTERED SHRIMP

MAKES 4 TO 6 SERVINGS

- ¾ cup mayonnaise
- ⅓ cup Thai sweet chili-garlic sauce
- 1¼ cups all-purpose flour
- 1 teaspoon baking powder
- ½ teaspoon sweet paprika
- ½ teaspoon salt
- 1 bottle (12 ounces) lager, as needed
- Vegetable oil for frying
- 1½ pounds raw shrimp, peeled and deveined

1 Combine mayonnaise and chili-garlic sauce in medium bowl; mix well. Cover; refrigerate at least 2 hours or up to 2 days.

2 Whisk flour, baking powder, paprika and salt in medium bowl. Whisk in enough lager to make thick batter. Cover; let stand at room temperature 2 to 4 hours.

3 Preheat oven to 200°F. Fill large heavy, deep saucepan half full with oil; heat over high heat to 350°F. Line large baking sheet with paper towels.

4 Working in batches, dip shrimp in batter, letting excess drip back into bowl. Carefully add shrimp to oil; cook 2½ minutes or until golden brown. Remove to prepared baking sheet with slotted spoon. Keep warm in oven while frying remaining shrimp. Serve warm with dip.

BEER-BRAISED MEATBALLS

MAKES 20 MEATBALLS

1 **pound ground beef**
½ **cup seasoned dry bread crumbs**
½ **cup grated Parmesan cheese**
2 **eggs, lightly beaten**
⅓ **cup finely chopped onion**
2 **cloves garlic, minced**
½ **teaspoon black pepper**
¼ **teaspoon salt**
1 **bottle (12 ounces) light-colored beer, such as lager**
1½ **cups tomato sauce**
1 **cup ketchup**
2 **tablespoons tomato paste**
½ **cup packed brown sugar**

1 Preheat oven to 400°F. Line broiler pan with foil; spray rack with nonstick cooking spray.

2 Combine beef, bread crumbs, cheese, eggs, onion, garlic, pepper and salt in large bowl; stir to blend. Shape mixture into 1-inch balls. Place meatballs on prepared pan. Bake 10 minutes or until browned.

3 Bring beer, tomato sauce, ketchup, tomato paste and brown sugar to a boil in Dutch oven. Add meatballs; reduce heat to medium-low. Cover; simmer 20 to 30 minutes or until meatballs are cooked through, stirring occasionally.

LAYERED BEER BEAN DIP

MAKES 4 TO 6 SERVINGS

1 can (about 15 ounces) pinto beans, rinsed and drained

1 can (12 ounces) beer

1½ cups chopped onions

3 cloves garlic, minced

2 teaspoons ground cumin

1 teaspoon dried oregano

1 teaspoon salt

1 cup guacamole

1 cup sour cream

1 cup salsa

½ cup chopped black olives

½ cup chopped green onions

1½ cups (6 ounces) shredded Cheddar or Monterey Jack cheese

Tortilla chips

1 Place beans in large saucepan over low heat. Add beer, onions, garlic, cumin, oregano and salt; simmer, stirring occasionally, 15 minutes or until no liquid remains. Remove from heat. Mash beans with potato masher or process in food processor. Set aside to cool.

2 Spread half of cooled beans in large dish or casserole that is at least 2 inches deep. Top with half of guacamole, half of sour cream, half of salsa, half of olives and half of green onions. Repeat layers and top with cheese. Serve with tortilla chips.

VARIATION

Use refried beans instead of whole beans. Place 15-ounce can of your favorite refried beans into small saucepan. Add 6 ounces of beer and simmer 10 minutes. If the refried beans are not seasoned, add garlic, cumin and oregano. Let cool and proceed.

BEEF AND BEER SLIDERS
MAKES 12 SLIDERS

- 6 tablespoons ketchup
- 2 tablespoons mayonnaise
- 2 teaspoons Dijon mustard
- 1½ pounds ground beef
- ½ cup beer
- 1 teaspoon salt
- ½ teaspoon garlic powder
- ½ teaspoon onion powder
- ½ teaspoon ground cumin
- ½ teaspoon dried oregano
- ¼ teaspoon black pepper
- 3 slices sharp Cheddar cheese, each cut into 4 pieces
- 12 slider buns or potato dinner rolls
- 12 baby lettuce leaves
- 12 plum tomato slices

1 Combine ketchup, mayonnaise and mustard in small bowl; reserve.

2 Combine beef, beer, salt, garlic powder, onion powder, cumin, oregano and pepper in medium bowl. Shape mixture into 12 (¼-inch-thick) patties.

3 Prepare grill for direct cooking over medium-high heat. Spray grid with cooking spray. Add half of patties; grill 2 minutes. Turn; top each with 1 piece cheese. Grill 2 minutes or until cheese is melted and patties are cooked through. Remove to large plate; keep warm. Repeat with remaining patties and cheese.

4 Serve sliders on rolls with ketchup mixture, lettuce and tomato.

BEER-FA-LO WINGS WITH BLUE CHEESE DIP

MAKES 10 TO 12 SERVINGS

Blue Cheese Dip (page 15)

5 pounds chicken wings, tips removed and split at joints

1 tablespoon olive oil

1 cup beer

½ cup hot pepper sauce

1 teaspoon Worcestershire sauce

6 tablespoons (¾ stick) unsalted butter

Celery and carrot sticks (optional)

1 Prepare Blue Cheese Dip. Preheat oven to 450°F. Spray large baking sheets with nonstick cooking spray.

2 Combine wings and oil in large bowl; toss to coat. Arrange wings on prepared baking sheets in single layer. Bake 40 to 45 minutes or until crisp and cooked through, rotating baking sheets halfway through baking time.

3 Meanwhile, combine beer, hot pepper sauce and Worcestershire sauce in small saucepan over medium-high heat. Bring to a boil; boil 12 to 14 minutes or until reduced to ½ cup. Remove from heat. Add butter; stir until melted.

4 Remove wings to another large bowl; add beer mixture and toss to coat. Remove to large serving platter. Serve with Blue Cheese Dip, celery and carrot sticks, if desired.

BLUE CHEESE DIP
MAKES ABOUT 2 CUPS

- 1 cup sour cream
- ½ cup mayonnaise
- ¾ cup crumbled blue cheese
- 1 teaspoon vinegar
- ¼ teaspoon salt
- ⅛ teaspoon black pepper

Combine sour cream, mayonnaise, blue cheese, vinegar, salt and pepper in small bowl; mix well. Refrigerate until ready to use.

BEER-BATTERED MUSHROOMS
MAKES 6 TO 8 SERVINGS

1½ quarts vegetable oil

1 cup all-purpose flour

½ teaspoon baking powder

½ teaspoon chili powder

¼ teaspoon salt, plus additional
   for seasoning

⅛ teaspoon black pepper

1 cup beer

1 egg, separated

1 pound small mushrooms

1   Heat oil in large saucepan to 365°F.
    Mix flour, baking powder, chili powder,
    ¼ teaspoon salt and pepper in medium
    bowl. Whisk beer and egg yolk in small
    bowl.

2   Beat egg white in medium bowl with
    electric mixer at medium speed until soft
    peaks form.

3   Stir beer mixture into flour mixture just
    until blended. Fold in egg white.

4   Dip mushrooms into batter in batches and
    carefully place in hot oil. Fry mushrooms,
    turning occasionally, until golden brown.
    (Stir batter and allow oil return to 365°F
    between batches.) Remove mushrooms to
    paper towels to drain; immediately season
    with additional salt. Serve warm.

LIME-BEER CHICKEN NACHOS
MAKES 6 TO 8 SERVINGS

1 cup beer

4 tablespoons fresh lime juice, divided

3 cloves garlic, minced

1 teaspoon ground cumin

¾ pound boneless skinless chicken thighs

1 pint grape tomatoes, halved

1 avocado, cut into ½-inch cubes

¼ cup finely chopped red onion

1 tablespoon chopped fresh cilantro

½ teaspoon salt, divided

¼ teaspoon black pepper

6 ounces restaurant-style tortilla chips

1 cup pasteurized process cheese spread

1 Combine beer, 3 tablespoons lime juice, garlic and cumin in medium bowl; stir to blend. Add chicken; toss to coat. Cover; refrigerate 1 hour or up to 4 hours.

2 Meanwhile, combine tomatoes, avocado, onion, cilantro, remaining 1 tablespoon lime juice and ¼ teaspoon salt in medium bowl; set aside.

3 Preheat oven to 400°F. Lightly oil grill pan and heat over medium-high heat. Remove chicken from beer marinade and sprinkle with remaining ¼ teaspoon salt and pepper. Add to grill pan and cook, turning once, 6 to 7 minutes per side or until thermometer inserted into thickest part of chicken registers 170°F. Remove to large cutting board and slice into thin strips.

4 Place tortilla chips on baking sheet. Bake 4 to 5 minutes or until heated through. Meanwhile, microwave cheese spread until heated through according to package directions.

5 Arrange half of tortilla chips on serving platter. Top with half of avocado mixture

and half of chicken strips. Drizzle with
half of melted cheese spread. Top with
remaining chips, avocado mixture,
chicken and cheese spread. Serve
immediately.

MINI BEER, BEEF & POTATO TURNOVERS

MAKES 18 TO 22 TURNOVERS

- 2 tablespoons olive oil
- 1½ cups chopped onions
- 2 cups chopped mushrooms
- ½ teaspoon salt
- ½ teaspoon dried thyme
- ⅛ teaspoon black pepper
- 1½ cups chopped cooked steak
- 1½ cups diced cooked baking potatoes
- 2 teaspoons Worcestershire sauce
- 1 cup dark beer
- All-purpose flour
- 2 packages (about 15 ounces each) refrigerated pie crusts (4 crusts)
- 1 egg
- 1 teaspoon water
- Beer Tarragon Mustard (page 21)

1 Preheat oven to 350°F. Spray two large baking sheets with nonstick cooking spray or line with parchment paper.

2 Heat oil in large skillet over medium heat. Add onions; cook and stir 5 minutes or until softened. Add mushrooms; cook and stir 5 to 6 minutes. Sprinkle with salt, thyme and pepper. Stir in steak, potatoes and Worcestershire sauce. Pour in beer. Increase heat to high; cook and stir 5 minutes or until liquid is absorbed. Remove from heat and let cool.

3 Sprinkle flour on large cutting board. Unroll pie crusts; cut out 4½-inch circles with biscuit or cookie cutter. Reroll scraps and cut out additional circles, repeating until all dough is used. Place on prepared baking sheets.

4 Place 2 tablespoons beef mixture in center of each circle. Fold dough over filling to make half moons; press edges with fork to seal. Prick tops with fork to vent. Whisk egg and water in small bowl; brush over turnovers.

5 Bake 25 to 30 minutes or until golden brown. Prepare Beer Tarragon Mustard; serve with turnovers.

BEER TARRAGON MUSTARD
MAKES ½ CUP MUSTARD

⅓ cup coarse grain mustard

2 tablespoons deli-style brown mustard

1 tablespoon chopped fresh tarragon

1 tablespoon beer

1 tablespoon honey

Combine all ingredients in small bowl; stir to blend. Cover; refrigerate until ready to serve.

ONION RING STACK

MAKES 4 TO 6 SERVINGS

1 cup all-purpose flour, divided

½ cup cornmeal

1 teaspoon black pepper

½ teaspoon salt, plus additional for seasoning

¼ to ½ teaspoon ground red pepper

1 cup light-colored beer

Remoulade Sauce (page 23) or ranch dressing

Vegetable oil for frying

6 tablespoons cornstarch, divided

2 large sweet onions, cut into ½-inch rings and separated

1 Combine ½ cup flour, cornmeal, black pepper, ½ teaspoon salt and red pepper in large bowl; mix well. Whisk in beer until well blended. Let stand 1 hour.

2 Prepare Remoulade Sauce; refrigerate until ready to serve.

3 Pour oil into large saucepan or Dutch oven to depth of 2 inches; heat to 360° to 370°F. Line large wire rack with paper towels.

4 Whisk 4 tablespoons cornstarch into batter. Combine remaining ½ cup flour and 2 tablespoons cornstarch in medium bowl. Thoroughly coat onions with flour mixture.

5 Working with one at a time, dip onion rings into batter to coat completely; carefully place in hot oil. Cook about 4 onion rings at a time 3 minutes or until golden brown, turning once. Remove to prepared wire rack; season with additional salt. Return oil to 370°F between batches. Serve immediately with Remoulade Sauce.

REMOULADE SAUCE

Combine 1 cup mayonnaise, 2 tablespoons coarse-grain mustard, 1 tablespoon lemon juice, 1 tablespoon sweet relish, 1 teaspoon horseradish sauce, 1 teaspoon Worcestershire sauce and ¼ teaspoon hot pepper sauce in medium bowl; mix well.

CHIPOTLE BEER FONDUE
MAKES 8 TO 10 SERVINGS

2 cups (8 ounces) shredded Swiss cheese

2 cups (8 ounces) shredded Colby-Jack cheese

1 cup (4 ounces) shredded Gouda cheese

1 tablespoon cornstarch

1 cup Mexican beer

1 clove garlic, minced

3 canned whole chipotle peppers in adobo sauce, minced

½ cup chopped green onions

⅛ teaspoon ground red pepper

Optional dippers: tortillas, French bread cubes, cauliflower florets, carrot slices and/or bell pepper slices

1 Toss Swiss, Colby-Jack and Gouda cheeses with cornstarch in large bowl; set aside.

2 Place beer and garlic in fondue pot or saucepan and bring to a boil over high heat. Reduce heat to low and slowly add cheese mixture, stirring constantly. Add chipotle peppers and green onions; cook and stir 2 to 3 minutes or until cheese is melted and mixture is smooth. Sprinkle with red pepper.

3 To serve, place fondue pot over low flame. Serve with desired dippers. Use fondue forks or skewers for dipping.

TIP

If you do not have a fondue pot, prepare the fondue in a saucepan and transfer to a heated slow cooker for serving.

COCONUT SHRIMP
MAKES 4 SERVINGS

Vegetable oil for frying

1¼ cups beer

¾ cup all-purpose flour

½ cup CREAM OF WHEAT® Hot Cereal (Instant, 1-minute, 2½-minute or 10-minute cook time), uncooked

2 teaspoons salt

2 teaspoons ground paprika

2 cups unsweetened shredded coconut, divided

1 pound uncooked shrimp, cleaned, peeled, deveined

Asian duck sauce or other dipping sauce (optional)

1 Preheat oil in deep fryer or heavy saucepan to 360°F. Combine beer, flour, Cream of Wheat, salt and paprika in medium bowl. Stir in 1 cup coconut; mix well. Let stand 5 minutes. Place remaining 1 cup coconut in shallow bowl.

2 Place shrimp into batter; stir to coat. Remove shrimp individually; dip each shrimp into coconut, covering evenly. Fry shrimp in batches 4 minutes or until golden brown. (Cook larger shrimp 1 to 2 minutes longer if necessary.) Remove with slotted spoon and drain on paper towels. Serve immediately with dipping sauce, if desired.

ON THE GRILL

APRICOT AND HONEY GLAZED BABY BACK RIBS

MAKES 6 TO 8 SERVINGS

- 1 tablespoon garlic powder
- 1 tablespoon ground cumin
- 1 teaspoon salt
- ½ teaspoon black pepper
- 6 pounds pork baby back ribs (2 racks), halved
- 1 bottle (12 ounces) honey wheat lager
- 1 cup apricot preserves
- 3 tablespoons honey

1 Prepare grill for indirect cooking over medium heat. Oil grid. Combine garlic powder, cumin, salt and pepper in small bowl. Rub over both sides of ribs.

2 Grill ribs, meat side down, over medium heat 30 minutes. Turn and grill 30 minutes.

3 Meanwhile, combine lager, preserves and honey in medium saucepan over medium-high heat. Bring to a boil; cook 20 minutes or until thick and reduced to ¾ cup.

4 Turn and brush ribs with half of glaze; grill 15 minutes. Turn and brush with remaining glaze; grill 15 minutes or until ribs are tender.

BEER-BASTED BARBECUE PORK CHOPS

MAKES 6 SERVINGS

- 1 cup prepared barbecue sauce, divided
- 1 cup plus 3 tablespoons beer, divided
- 3 tablespoons honey
- 1 tablespoon chili powder
- 6 bone-in loin pork chops, cut about 1 inch thick
- 1 teaspoon salt
- ½ teaspoon black pepper

1 Combine ½ cup barbecue sauce, 1 cup beer, honey and chili powder in large bowl. Add pork chops, turning to coat; refrigerate 2 to 4 hours, turning occasionally. Combine remaining ½ cup barbecue sauce and 3 tablespoons beer in separate bowl; set aside.

2 Prepare grill for direct cooking over medium-high heat. Oil grid.

3 Remove pork chops from beer mixture and sprinkle with salt and pepper. Place pork chops on prepared grid over medium-high heat. Grill 4 minutes. Turn chops over; brush with half of reserved barbecue sauce mixture. Grill 3 minutes. Turn over; brush with remaining sauce mixture and grill 4 to 5 minutes or until an instant read thermometer inserted into the thickest portion of pork chops registers 150°F.

GRILLED PIZZA MARGHERITA WITH BEER-RISEN CRUST

MAKES 4 SERVINGS

- ¾ cup beer
- 1 package (¼ ounce) active dry yeast
- 2 tablespoons plus 2 teaspoons extra virgin olive oil, divided
- 1¾ to 2½ cups all-purpose flour
- 1⅛ teaspoons salt, divided
- 1½ pints grape tomatoes, halved
- 1 clove garlic, minced
- ¼ teaspoon dried basil
- ⅛ teaspoon red pepper flakes
- 6 ounces fresh mozzarella, cut into 12 slices
- 10 fresh basil leaves, thinly sliced

1 Microwave beer in small microwavable bowl on HIGH 25 seconds. Stir in yeast and 2 teaspoons oil; let stand 5 minutes or until foamy. Combine 1¾ cups flour and 1 teaspoon salt in medium bowl. Add beer mixture to flour mixture and stir until dough pulls away from side of bowl, adding additional flour as needed. Turn out dough onto lightly floured surface; knead 6 to 7 minutes, adding enough additional flour to make smooth and elastic dough. Divide dough in half and form into balls. Dust with flour; place in separate medium bowls. Cover; let rise in warm, draft-free place about 1½ hours or until doubled in size.

2 Heat 1 tablespoon oil in medium skillet over medium-high heat. Add tomatoes, garlic, basil, remaining ⅛ teaspoon salt and red pepper flakes; cook 3 to 4 minutes or until tomatoes are very soft, stirring occasionally. Set aside.

3 Prepare grill for direct cooking over high heat. Oil grid.

4 Working with one dough ball at a time, turn dough onto lightly floured surface. Gently stretch dough into 9-inch round. Transfer to floured baking sheets. Brush tops of each round with half of remaining oil. Cover and let stand 10 minutes.

5 *Reduce grill to medium heat.* Carefully flip dough rounds onto grid, oiled side down. Grill, uncovered, 3 minutes or until bottoms are golden and well marked. Turn crusts; spread with tomato mixture, leaving ½-inch border. Top with cheese; cover and grill 3 minutes or until cheese begins to melt and crusts are golden brown. Remove to large cutting board; sprinkle with basil.

CHEDDAR-BEER BURGERS WITH BACON

MAKES 4 SERVINGS

1½ pounds ground beef

4 ounces sharp Cheddar cheese, cut into ½-inch cubes

½ cup beer

¼ cup chopped fresh parsley

1 teaspoon paprika

¾ teaspoon garlic powder

¾ teaspoon salt

¼ teaspoon black pepper

¼ cup ketchup

2 tablespoons mayonnaise

4 hamburger buns

4 lettuce leaves

4 slices tomato

4 thick slices red onion

8 slices bacon, cooked

1 Prepare grill for direct cooking over medium-high heat.

2 Combine beef, cheese, beer, parsley, paprika, garlic powder, salt and pepper in large bowl; stir to blend. Shape into four patties, making centers of patties slightly thinner than edges.

3 Grill patties, covered, 8 to 10 minutes (or uncovered, 13 to 15 minutes) to medium (160°F) or to desired doneness, turning once.

4 Meanwhile, combine ketchup and mayonnaise in small bowl; stir to blend. Top bottom half of each bun with ketchup mixture, lettuce leaf, tomato slice, onion slice, burger and bacon; cover with top halves of buns.

BEER AND ORANGE MARINATED TUNA STEAKS

MAKES 4 SERVINGS

NECTARINE SALSA

2 large nectarines, pitted and diced

3 tablespoons finely chopped red onion

½ jalapeño pepper, finely chopped

2 tablespoons fresh chopped cilantro

1 tablespoon lime juice

¼ teaspoon salt

TUNA

½ cup beer

⅓ cup chopped green onions

¼ cup orange juice

¼ cup reduced-sodium soy sauce

2 tablespoons lemon juice

2 tablespoons grated fresh ginger

2 cloves garlic, minced

2 tablespoons sugar

4 (6- to 8-ounce) tuna steaks, about ¾ inch thick

1 For salsa, combine nectarines, onion, jalapeño, cilantro, lime juice and salt in medium bowl.

2 For tuna, combine beer, green onions, orange juice, soy sauce, lemon juice, ginger, garlic and sugar in large bowl; mix well. Add tuna, turning to coat. Refrigerate 30 minutes, turning occasionally.

3 Prepare grill for direct cooking over medium-high heat.

4 Remove tuna from marinade; place on oiled grid. Grill tuna 3 minutes per side or until marked and pink in center. Remove to serving plates. Serve with salsa.

CHIPOTLE SPICE-RUBBED BEER CAN CHICKEN

MAKES 4 SERVINGS

2 tablespoons packed brown sugar

2 teaspoons smoked paprika

2 teaspoons ground cumin

1 teaspoon salt

1 teaspoon garlic powder

1 teaspoon chili powder

½ teaspoon ground chipotle pepper

1 whole chicken (3½ to 4 pounds), rinsed and patted dry

1 can (12 ounces) beer

1 Prepare grill for indirect cooking over medium heat.

2 Combine brown sugar, paprika, cumin, salt, garlic powder, chili powder and chipotle pepper in small bowl; stir to blend. Gently loosen skin of chicken over breast, legs and thighs. Rub sugar mixture under and over skin and inside cavity. Discard one fourth of beer. Hold chicken upright with cavity pointing down; insert beer can into cavity.

3 Oil grid. Place chicken on grid, standing upright on can. Spread legs slightly for support. Grill, covered, 1 hour 15 minutes or until chicken is cooked through (165°F).

4 Lift chicken off beer can using metal tongs. Let rest upright on large cutting board 5 minutes before carving.

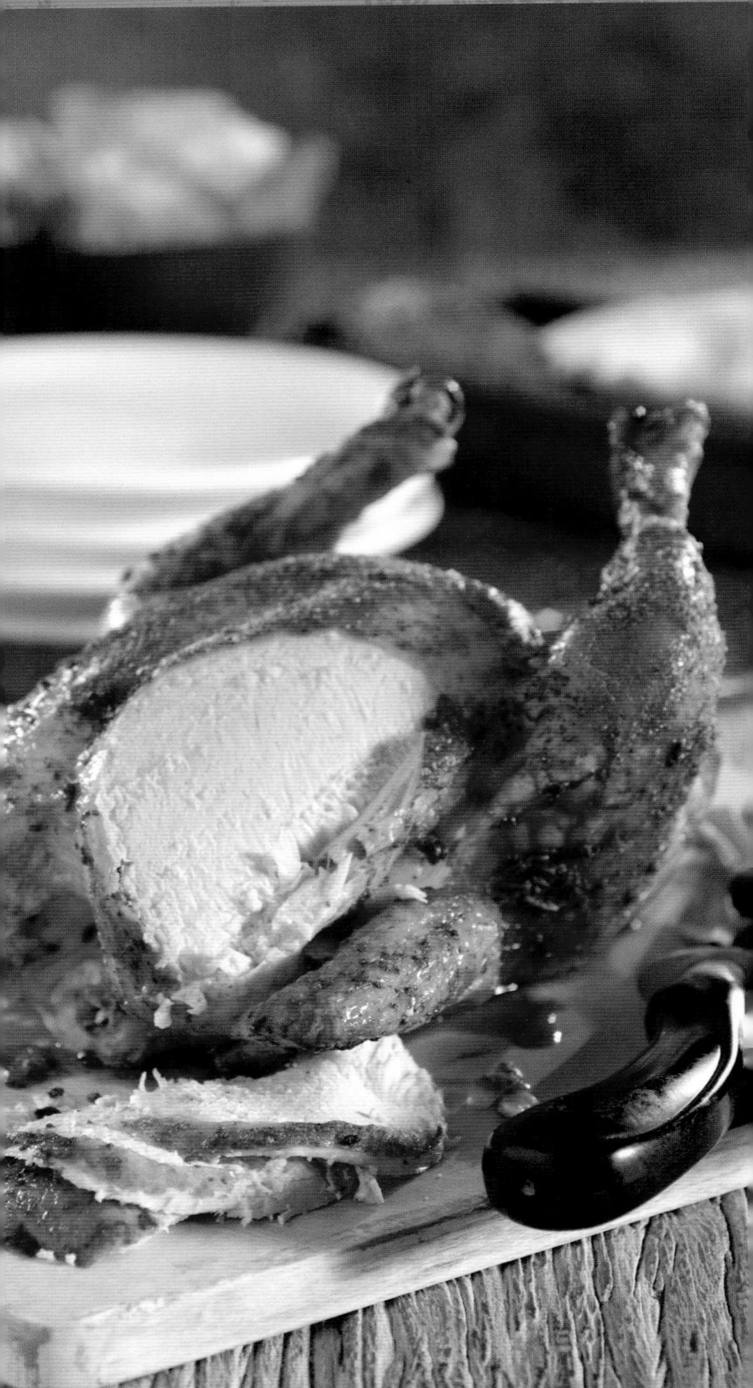

BEER-MARINATED STEAK
MAKES 3 TO 4 SERVINGS

- 1 cup beer*
- 1 onion, finely chopped
- ½ cup soy sauce
- ¼ teaspoon black pepper
- 1½ pounds boneless beef top sirloin steak (¾ inch thick)
- ¼ cup (1 ounce) shredded Cheddar cheese (optional)

Do not use reduced-calorie light beer.

1 Combine beer, onion, soy sauce and pepper in medium bowl. Place steak in large resealable food storage bag; add beer mixture. Seal bag; turn to coat steak. Refrigerate at least 8 hours or overnight, turning occasionally.

2 Prepare grill for direct cooking over medium-high heat or preheat broiler.

3 Drain steak, discarding marinade. Grill, covered, 4 to 5 minutes per side for medium rare (145°F) or to desired doneness. If desired, sprinkle steak evenly with cheese just before removing from grill. Cut into thin slices across the grain.

SERVING SUGGESTION

Serve with sautéed vegetables and cilantro-lime rice. For vegetables, thinly slice one of each red onion, red bell pepper and green bell pepper. Heat 1 tablespoon oil in large skillet over high heat. Add vegetables; cook and stir 5 minutes or until softened and browned. For rice, stir ¼ cup chopped fresh cilantro and 2 tablespoons lime juice into 3 cups of hot cooked rice. Season to taste with salt.

WESTERN BARBECUE BURGERS WITH BEER BARBECUE SAUCE

MAKES 4 SERVINGS

1½ pounds ground beef

1 cup smokehouse-style barbecue sauce

¼ cup brown ale

½ teaspoon salt

¼ teaspoon black pepper

1 red onion, cut into ½-inch-thick slices

4 hamburger buns

8 slices thick-cut bacon, crisp-cooked

Lettuce leaves

Tomato slices

1 Prepare grill for direct cooking over medium-high heat. Shape beef into four patties about ¾ inch thick.

2 Combine barbecue sauce, ale, salt and pepper in small saucepan. Bring to a boil; boil 1 minute. Set aside.

3 Grill burgers, covered, 8 to 10 minutes or to desired doneness, turning occasionally. Grill onion 4 minutes or until softened and slightly charred, turning occasionally.

4 Serve burgers on buns with onion, bacon, barbecue sauce mixture, lettuce and tomatoes.

GRILLED SALMON WITH PINEAPPLE SALSA

MAKES 4 SERVINGS

- ½ pineapple, cut into ½-inch cubes (about 2 cups)
- ½ cup Mexican beer
- 1 tablespoon sugar
- ¼ cup finely chopped red onion
- ¼ cup finely chopped red bell pepper
- 2 tablespoons chopped fresh cilantro
- 1 tablespoon lime juice
- 1 teaspoon salt, divided
- 4 salmon fillets (6 to 8 ounces each)
- 1 tablespoon olive oil
- ¼ teaspoon black pepper

1 Combine pineapple, beer and sugar in medium bowl; refrigerate 1 hour. Drain and discard all but 2 tablespoons liquid. Add onion, bell pepper, cilantro, lime juice and ½ teaspoon salt to pineapple mixture; refrigerate 1 hour or overnight.

2 Prepare grill for direct cooking over medium-high heat. Lightly oil grid. Rub salmon fillets with oil; sprinkle with remaining ½ teaspoon salt and black pepper.

3 Grill 5 minutes per side or until salmon just begins to flake when tested with fork. Serve salmon with salsa.

CHICKEN AND VEGETABLE SATAY WITH PEANUT SAUCE

MAKES 4 SERVINGS

- 1½ pounds boneless skinless chicken thighs, cut into 32 (1½-inch) cubes
- ⅔ cup Thai or other Asian beer, divided
- 3 tablespoons packed dark brown sugar, divided
- 1 tablespoon plus 2 teaspoons lime juice, divided
- 3 cloves garlic, minced and divided
- 1¼ teaspoons curry powder, divided
- ½ cup coconut milk
- ½ cup chunky peanut butter
- 1 tablespoon fish sauce
- 3 tablespoons peanut oil, divided
- ¼ cup finely chopped onion
- 24 medium mushrooms, stems trimmed
- 4 green onions, cut into 24 (1-inch) pieces
- Hot cooked noodles or rice (optional)

1 Place chicken in large resealable food storage bag. Combine chicken, ⅓ cup beer, 1 tablespoon brown sugar, 1 tablespoon lime juice, 2 cloves garlic and 1 teaspoon curry powder in small bowl. Pour over chicken. Seal bag; turn to coat. Refrigerate 2 hours, turning occasionally.

2 Meanwhile, combine remaining ⅓ cup beer, 2 tablespoons brown sugar, 2 teaspoons lime juice, coconut milk, peanut butter and fish sauce in medium bowl. Heat 1 tablespoon oil in small saucepan over medium-high heat. Add chopped onion and remaining clove garlic; cook 2 to 3 minutes or just until starting to soften. Add remaining ¼ teaspoon curry powder; cook 15 seconds. Stir in coconut milk mixture. Reduce heat to medium and simmer 15 minutes or until thickened, stirring frequently. Keep warm.

3 Prepare grill for direct cooking over medium-high heat. Remove chicken from marinade; discard marinade. Alternately thread chicken, mushrooms and green onions onto eight skewers. Lightly oil grid. Brush skewers with remaining 2 tablespoons oil. Grill 8 to 10 minutes, turning occasionally, until chicken is cooked through and mushrooms are tender. Serve with peanut sauce. For a heartier meal, serve over noodles or rice, if desired.

GRILLED CHICKEN SANDWICHES WITH BEER-BRAISED ONIONS

MAKES 4 SERVINGS

- 4 boneless skinless chicken breasts (5 to 6 ounces each), pounded slightly
- ½ cup lager
- 3 tablespoons Dijon mustard
- 1 tablespoon paprika
- 1 tablespoon olive oil
- 2 cloves garlic, minced
- 1 teaspoon dried basil
- ¾ teaspoon salt
- ¼ teaspoon black pepper
- 4 English muffins or sandwich rolls, toasted

  Beer-Braised Onions (page 49)

1 Combine chicken, lager, mustard, paprika, oil, garlic and basil in large resealable food storage bag. Seal bag; turn to coat. Refrigerate 2 hours, turning occasionally.

2 Prepare grill for direct cooking. Oil grid.

3 Drain chicken, discarding marinade. Season chicken with salt and pepper. Grill chicken, covered, over medium heat 4 to 6 minutes per side or until no longer pink in center.

4 Meanwhile, prepare Beer-Braised Onions. Serve chicken on English muffins with Beer-Braised Onions.

BEER-BRAISED ONIONS
MAKES ½ CUP

1 tablespoon butter

1½ cups thinly sliced red onion (about 1 medium onion)

2 tablespoons sugar

2 tablespoons lager

1 tablespoon balsamic vinegar

¼ teaspoon salt

Melt butter in medium nonstick skillet over medium heat. Add onion and sugar; cook 5 to 7 minutes or until onion is soft but not browned, stirring occasionally. Stir in lager, vinegar and salt; cook 1 minute or until liquid evaporates.

TEXAS SMOKED BBQ BRISKET

MAKES 10 TO 12 SERVINGS

- ½ cup prepared barbecue seasoning
- 2 tablespoons ground chili powder
- 1 (5- to 7-pound) beef brisket, trimmed with a layer of fat (center flat portion)
- 1 cup **FRANK'S**® **RedHot**® Original Cayenne Pepper Sauce
- 1½ cups beer *or* non-alcoholic malt beverage, divided
- 1 cup *Cattlemen's*® Authentic Smoke House Barbecue Sauce *or* *Cattlemen's*® Award Winning Classic Barbecue Sauce
- ¼ cup (½ stick) butter

COMBINE barbecue seasoning and chili powder. Rub mixture thoroughly into beef. Place meat, fat-side up, into disposable foil pan. Cover and refrigerate 1 to 3 hours. Just before using, prepare mop sauce by combining **FRANK'S**® **RedHot**® Original Cayenne Pepper Sauce and *1 cup* beer; set aside.

PREPARE grill for indirect cooking over medium-low heat (250°F). If desired, toss soaked wood chips over coals or heat source. Place pan with meat in center of grill over indirect heat. Cover grill. Cook meat over low heat 6 to 7 hours until meat is very tender (190°F internal temperature). Baste with mop sauce once an hour.

COMBINE barbecue sauce, butter and remaining *½ cup* beer. Simmer 5 minutes until slightly thickened. Slice meat and serve with sauce.

TIP

To easily slice meat, cut against the grain using an electric knife.

BEER-BRINED GRILLED PORK CHOPS
MAKES 4 SERVINGS

1 bottle (12 ounces) dark beer

¼ cup packed dark brown sugar

1 tablespoon salt

1 tablespoon chili powder

2 cloves garlic, minced

3 cups ice water

4 pork chops (1 inch thick)

Grilled Rosemary Potatoes (recipe follows)

1 Whisk beer, brown sugar, salt, chili powder and garlic in medium bowl until salt is dissolved. Add ice water and stir until ice melts. Add pork chops; place medium plate on top to keep chops submerged in brine. Refrigerate 3 to 4 hours.

2 Prepare grill for direct cooking over medium heat. Drain pork chops and pat dry with paper towels. Prepare Grilled Rosemary Potatoes. Grill pork chops, covered, 10 to 12 minutes. Serve with potatoes.

GRILLED ROSEMARY POTATOES

Place 4 quartered potatoes, ¼ cup chopped onion, 2 teaspoons chopped fresh rosemary and 1 teaspoon red pepper flakes on a 13×9-inch piece of foil. Toss mixture on foil; top with an additional 13×9-inch piece of foil. Seal edges of foil pieces together to make a packet. Grill 12 to 15 minutes or until potatoes are tender. Makes 4 servings.

TIP

Brining adds flavor and moisture to meats. Be sure that your pork chops have not been injected with a sodium solution (check the package label) or they could end up too salty.

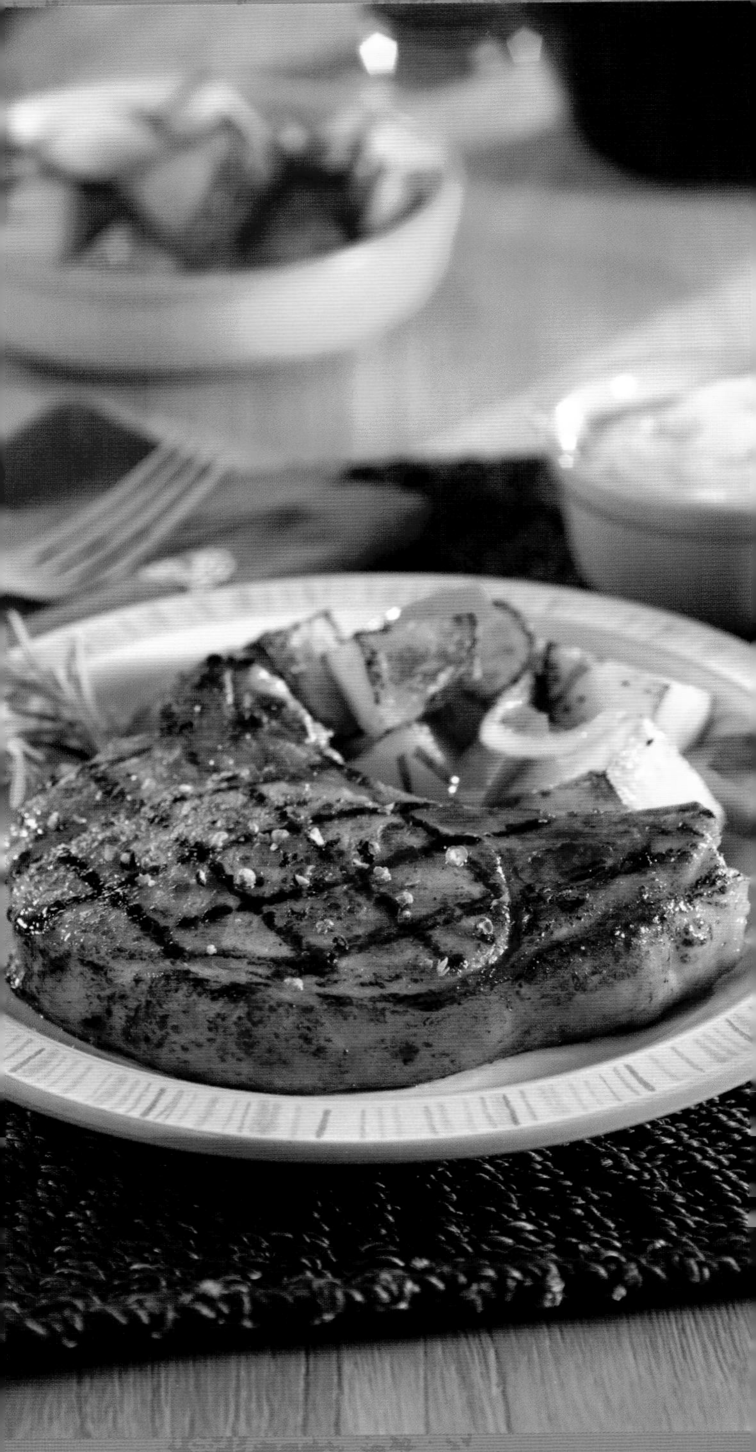

GRILLED SKIRT STEAK FAJITAS

MAKES 4 SERVINGS

- 1½ pounds skirt steak
- ½ cup pale ale
- 3 tablespoons lime juice
- 1 teaspoon ground cumin
- 2 tablespoons olive oil
- 1 cup thinly sliced red onion
- 1 cup thinly sliced red and green bell peppers
- 2 cloves garlic, minced
- 3 plum tomatoes, each cut into 4 wedges
- 1 tablespoon reduced-sodium soy sauce
- ¾ teaspoon salt
- ¼ teaspoon black pepper
- 8 (7-inch) flour tortillas
- Avocado slices and salsa (optional)

1 Place steak in large resealable food storage bag. Combine ale, lime juice and cumin in small bowl; pour over steak. Seal bag; turn to coat. Refrigerate 2 hours, turning occasionally.

2 Heat oil in large skillet over medium-high heat. Add onion; cook and stir 2 to 3 minutes or until beginning to soften. Add bell peppers; cook and stir 7 to 8 minutes or until softened. Add garlic; cook and stir 1 minute. Add tomatoes; cook 2 minutes or just until beginning to soften. Add soy sauce; cook 1 minute. Keep warm.

3 Prepare grill for direct cooking over medium-high heat. Lightly oil grid.

4 Remove steak from marinade; discard marinade. Sprinkle with salt and black pepper. Grill 4 to 6 minutes on each side to 145°F or desired doneness. Remove to large cutting board; cut across grain into ¼-inch-thick slices.

5 Warm tortillas and fill with steak and vegetable mixture. Top with avocado slices and salsa, if desired.

SOUPS, STEWS AND CHILIS

SPLIT PEA SOUP WITH HAM AND ALE

MAKES 6 SERVINGS

1 tablespoon olive oil

1 cup chopped onion

½ cup chopped carrot

½ cup chopped celery

3 cloves garlic, minced

1 bay leaf

¼ teaspoon dried thyme

1 bottle (12 ounces) Belgian white ale

4 cups chicken broth

1 package (16 ounces) dried split peas, rinsed and sorted

1 pound smoked ham hocks

2 cups water

1 Heat oil in Dutch oven over medium heat. Add onion, carrot, celery, garlic, bay leaf and thyme; cook 4 to 5 minutes or until vegetables begin to soften, stirring occasionally. Add ale; bring to boil over medium-high heat. Cook 6 to 7 minutes or until ale is reduced by half.

2 Stir in broth, split peas, ham hocks and water; bring to a boil. Reduce heat to medium-low; cover and simmer 1 hour or until split peas are tender, stirring occasionally.

3 Remove ham hocks to large cutting board; let stand until cool enough to handle. Remove ham from hocks. Chop ham and stir into Dutch oven. Remove and discard bay leaf.

CHEESY TAVERN SOUP

MAKES 8 SERVINGS

- 2 tablespoons olive oil
- ½ cup chopped celery
- ½ cup chopped carrot
- ½ cup chopped onion
- ½ cup chopped green bell pepper
- 8 cups chicken broth
- 2 cans (12 ounces *each*) beer, at room temperature
- ¼ cup (½ stick) butter
- 2 teaspoons salt
- 2 teaspoons black pepper
- ½ cup all-purpose flour
- 4 cups (16 ounces) shredded Cheddar cheese
- Sliced green onions (optional)

SLOW COOKER DIRECTIONS

1 Heat oil in medium skillet over medium heat. Add celery, carrot, chopped onion and bell pepper; cook and stir 3 minutes or until tender. Remove to **CROCK-POT®** slow cooker.

2 Add broth, beer, butter, salt and black pepper to **CROCK-POT®** slow cooker. Cover; cook on LOW 6 hours or on HIGH 2 to 4 hours.

3 Stir small amount of water into flour in small bowl until smooth. Whisk into **CROCK-POT®** slow cooker. Cover; cook on HIGH 10 to 15 minutes or until thickened.

4 Preheat broiler. Ladle soup into individual broiler-safe bowls. Top each with ½ cup cheese. Broil 10 to 15 minutes or until cheese is melted. Garnish with green onions.

HEARTY PORK AND BACON CHILI

MAKES 8 TO 10 SERVINGS

2½ pounds boneless pork shoulder, cut into 1-inch pieces

3½ teaspoons salt, divided

1¼ teaspoons black pepper, divided

1 tablespoon vegetable oil

4 slices thick-cut bacon, diced

2 medium onions, chopped

1 red bell pepper, chopped

¼ cup chili powder

2 tablespoons tomato paste

1 tablespoon minced garlic

1 tablespoon ground cumin

1 tablespoon smoked paprika

1 bottle (12 ounces) pale ale

2 cans (about 14 ounces *each*) diced tomatoes

2 cups water

¾ cup dried kidney beans, rinsed and sorted

¾ cup dried black beans, rinsed and sorted

3 tablespoons cornmeal

Feta cheese and chopped fresh cilantro (optional)

SLOW COOKER DIRECTIONS

1 Season pork with 1 teaspoon salt and 1 teaspoon black pepper. Heat oil in large skillet over medium-high heat. Add pork in batches; cook 6 minutes or until browned on all sides. Remove to slow cooker using slotted spoon.

2 Heat same skillet over medium heat. Add bacon; cook and stir until crisp. Remove to slow cooker using slotted spoon.

3 Pour off all but 2 tablespoons drippings from skillet. Return skillet to medium heat. Add onions and bell pepper; cook and

stir 6 minutes or just until softened. Stir in chili powder, tomato paste, garlic, cumin, paprika, remaining 2½ teaspoons salt and remaining ¼ teaspoon black pepper; cook and stir 1 minute. Stir in ale. Bring to a simmer, scraping up any browned bits from bottom of skillet. Pour over pork in slow cooker. Stir in tomatoes, water, beans and cornmeal.

4 Cover; cook on LOW 10 hours. Turn off heat. Let stand 10 minutes. Skim fat from surface. Garnish each serving with cheese and cilantro.

SOUTHWEST ONION SOUP

MAKES 8 SERVINGS

1 tablespoon olive oil

2 large Spanish onions, sliced

1 boneless beef chuck roast
  (about ½ pound), cut into cubes

1 teaspoon ground chipotle chile pepper

4 cups SWANSON® Beef Broth (Regular,
  50% Less Sodium **or** Certified
  Organic)

1 bottle (12 fluid ounces) Mexican beer

1 can (about 14.5 ounces) diced
  tomatoes with jalapeños

1 cup frozen or drained, canned whole
  kernel corn

  Tortilla chips

1 package (8 ounces) shredded Mexican
  cheese blend (2 cups)

1 Heat the oil in a 6-quart saucepot over
  medium-high heat. Add the onions and
  cook until they're tender.

2 Add the beef and pepper. Cook until the
  beef is well browned, stirring often.

3 Stir the broth, beer, tomatoes and corn in
  the saucepot. Heat to a boil. Reduce the
  heat to low. Cover and cook for 15 minutes
  or until the beef is fork-tender.

4 Divide the soup among **8** microwavable
  serving bowls. Top **each** with **3** tortilla
  chips and **2 tablespoons** of the cheese.
  Microwave **2** bowls at a time on HIGH for
  30 seconds or until the cheese melts.
  Serve immediately.

IRISH LAMB STEW
MAKES 8 SERVINGS

½ cup all-purpose flour

2 teaspoons salt, divided

½ teaspoon black pepper, divided

3 pounds boneless lamb stew meat, cut into 1½-inch cubes

3 tablespoons vegetable oil

1 cup chopped onion

1 can (about 15 ounces) Irish stout, divided

1 teaspoon sugar

1 teaspoon dried thyme

1 pound unpeeled small new potatoes, quartered

1 pound carrots, peeled and cut into ½-inch pieces

½ cup water

1 cup frozen peas

¼ cup chopped fresh parsley

1 Combine flour, 1 teaspoon salt and ¼ teaspoon pepper in large bowl. Add lamb; toss to coat, shaking off excess. Discard any remaining flour mixture.

2 Heat oil in Dutch oven over medium heat. Cook lamb in batches 7 minutes or until browned on all sides. Remove to bowl.

3 Add onion and ¼ cup stout to Dutch oven; cook 10 minutes, scraping up any browned bits from bottom of pan. Return lamb to Dutch oven; stir in remaining stout, 1 teaspoon salt, ¼ teaspoon pepper, sugar and thyme. If necessary, add enough water so liquid just covers lamb. Bring to a boil over medium-high heat. Reduce heat to low; cover and simmer 1½ hours or until lamb is tender.

4 Stir in potatoes, carrots and ½ cup water; cover and cook 30 minutes or until vegetables are tender. Stir in peas and parsley; cook 5 to 10 minutes or until heated through.

BEER-BRAISED CHILI
MAKES ABOUT 8 CUPS

- 2 tablespoons canola or vegetable oil
- 2 pounds boneless beef chuck roast or stew meat, cut into ¾-inch cubes
- 1 large onion, chopped
- 4 cloves garlic, minced
- 1 tablespoon chili powder
- 1 tablespoon ground cumin
- 1¼ teaspoons salt
- 1 teaspoon dried oregano
- ½ teaspoon ground red pepper
- 1 can (about 14 ounces) Mexican-style stewed tomatoes, undrained
- 1 bottle or can (12 ounces) beer (not dark beer)
- ½ cup salsa
- 1 can (about 15 ounces) black beans, rinsed and drained
- 1 can (about 15 ounces) red beans or pinto beans, rinsed and drained

  Optional toppings: chopped fresh cilantro, thinly sliced green onions, shredded Chihuahua or Cheddar cheese, sliced pickled jalapeño peppers, sour cream

1 Heat oil in large saucepan or Dutch oven over medium-high heat. Add beef, onion and garlic; cook 5 minutes, stirring occasionally. Sprinkle with chili powder, cumin, salt, oregano and ground red pepper; mix well. Add tomatoes, beer and salsa; bring to a boil. Reduce heat; cover and simmer 1¼ hours or until beef is very tender, stirring once.

2 Stir in beans. Simmer, uncovered, 20 minutes or until thickened as desired. Serve with desired toppings.

BEEF AND BREW STEW

MAKES 8 SERVINGS

- 3 tablespoons vegetable oil
- 3 pounds boneless beef chuck roast, cut into 1-inch pieces
- 2 large onions, sliced (about 2 cups)
- 2 cloves garlic, minced
- 2 cans (10¾ ounces **each**) CAMPBELL'S® Condensed Golden Mushroom Soup
- 2 cans (10½ ounces **each**) CAMPBELL'S® Condensed French Onion Soup
- 1 bottle (12 fluid ounces) dark beer **or** stout
- 1 tablespoon packed brown sugar
- 1 tablespoon cider vinegar
- ½ teaspoon dried thyme leaves, crushed
- 1 bay leaf
- 2 cups fresh **or** frozen whole baby carrots

  Egg noodles, cooked, drained and buttered

1 Heat **1 tablespoon** oil in an oven-safe 6-quart saucepot over medium-high heat. Add the beef in 3 batches and cook until well browned, stirring often, adding an additional **1 tablespoon** oil as needed during cooking. Remove the beef from the saucepot. Pour off any fat.

2 Heat the remaining oil in the saucepot over medium heat. Add the onions and garlic and cook until the onions are tender.

3 Stir the soups, beer, brown sugar, vinegar, thyme, bay leaf and carrots in the saucepot and heat to a boil. Cover the saucepot.

4 Bake at 300°F. for 2 hours or until the beef is fork-tender. Discard the bay leaf. Serve the beef mixture over the noodles.

CHICKEN AND SAUSAGE GUMBO WITH BEER

MAKES 6 SERVINGS

- ½ cup all-purpose flour
- ½ cup vegetable oil
- 4½ cups chicken broth
- 1 bottle (12 ounces) beer
- 3 pounds boneless skinless chicken thighs
- 1½ teaspoons salt, divided
- ½ teaspoon garlic powder
- ¾ teaspoon ground red pepper, divided
- 1 pound fully cooked andouille sausage, sliced into rounds
- 1 large onion, chopped
- ½ red bell pepper, chopped
- ½ green bell pepper, chopped
- 2 stalks celery, chopped
- 2 cloves garlic, minced
- 2 bay leaves
- ½ teaspoon black pepper
- 3 cups hot cooked rice
- ½ cup sliced green onions
- 1 teaspoon filé powder (optional)

1 Add flour and oil to Dutch oven; cook and stir over medium-low heat 20 minutes or until mixture is caramel colored. (Once mixture begins to darken, watch carefully to avoid burning.)

2 Meanwhile, heat broth and beer in medium saucepan to a simmer. Keep warm over low heat. Season chicken with ½ teaspoon salt, garlic powder and ¼ teaspoon ground red pepper.

3 Add chicken, sausage, onion, bell peppers, celery, garlic, bay leaves, black pepper, remaining 1 teaspoon salt and ½ teaspoon ground red pepper to Dutch oven; stir well. Gradually add hot broth mixture, stirring

constantly to prevent lumps. Bring to a simmer. Cover and simmer 1 to 2 hours.

4 Remove and discard bay leaves. Place ½ cup rice in each of six bowls; top with gumbo. Sprinkle with green onions and filé powder, if desired, before serving.

DEVILED BEEF SHORT RIB STEW

MAKES 6 SERVINGS (WITH 3 CUPS GRAVY)

4 pounds beef short ribs, trimmed

2 pounds small red potatoes, scrubbed and scored

8 carrots, peeled and cut into chunks

2 onions, cut into thick wedges

1 bottle (12 ounces) beer or non-alcoholic malt beverage

8 tablespoons FRENCH'S® Spicy Brown Mustard, divided

3 tablespoons FRENCH'S® Worcestershire Sauce, divided

2 tablespoons cornstarch

SLOW COOKER DIRECTIONS

1 Broil ribs 6 inches from heat on rack in broiler pan 10 minutes or until well browned, turning once. Place vegetables in bottom of slow cooker. Place ribs on top of vegetables.

2 Combine beer, *6 tablespoons* mustard and *2 tablespoons* Worcestershire in medium bowl. Pour into slow cooker. Cover and cook on HIGH setting for 5 hours* or until meat is tender.

3 Transfer meat and vegetables to platter; keep warm. Strain fat from broth; pour broth into saucepan. Combine cornstarch with *2 tablespoons cold water* in small bowl. Stir into broth with remaining *2 tablespoons* mustard and *1 tablespoon* Worcestershire. Heat to boiling. Reduce heat to medium-low. Cook 1 to 2 minutes or until thickened, stirring often. Pass gravy with meat and vegetables. Serve meat with additional mustard.

Or cook 10 hours on LOW setting.

TIP

Use a spiced winter ale in this stew for an even bolder beef flavor.

CHILE VERDE CHICKEN STEW

MAKES 6 SERVINGS

⅓ cup all-purpose flour

1½ teaspoons salt, divided

¼ teaspoon black pepper

1½ pounds boneless skinless chicken breasts, cut into 1½-inch pieces

4 tablespoons vegetable oil, divided

1 pound tomatillos (about 9), husked and halved

2 onions, chopped

2 cans (4 ounces each) diced mild green chiles

1 tablespoon dried oregano

1 tablespoon ground cumin

2 cloves garlic, chopped

1 teaspoon sugar

2 cups reduced-sodium chicken broth

8 ounces Mexican beer

5 unpeeled red potatoes, diced

Optional toppings: chopped fresh cilantro, sour cream, shredded Monterey Jack cheese, lime wedges, diced avocado and/or hot pepper sauce

1 Combine flour, 1 teaspoon salt and pepper in large bowl. Add chicken; toss to coat. Heat 2 tablespoons oil in large skillet over medium heat. Add chicken; cook 5 to 8 minutes or until lightly browned on all sides. Remove to Dutch oven.

2 Heat remaining 2 tablespoons oil in same skillet. Add tomatillos, onions, chiles, oregano, cumin, garlic, sugar and remaining ½ teaspoon salt; cook and stir 20 minutes or until vegetables are softened. Stir in broth and beer. Working in batches, process mixture in food processor or blender until almost smooth.

3 Add mixture to chicken in Dutch oven. Stir in potatoes. Cover; bring to a boil over medium-high heat. Reduce heat to low; simmer 1 hour or until potatoes are tender, stirring occasionally. Serve with desired toppings.

VARIATION

Omit potato and serve over hot white rice.

FARMER'S MARKET GRILLED CHOWDER

MAKES 4 SERVINGS

- 1 ear corn
- 1 large potato
- 1 small zucchini, cut lengthwise into ¼-inch-thick slices
- 1 tablespoon butter
- ½ cup chopped onion
- 2 tablespoons all-purpose flour
- ½ teaspoon salt
- ½ teaspoon dried thyme
- ⅛ teaspoon white pepper
- 1 cup wheat beer
- 1 cup milk
- ½ cup (2 ounces) shredded sharp Cheddar cheese

1. Prepare grill for direct cooking over medium-high heat. Remove husks and silk from corn. Cut potato in half lengthwise. Grill corn and potato, covered, 20 minutes or until tender, turning once. Remove kernels from cob. Cut potato into cubes. Set aside.

2. Spray zucchini with nonstick cooking spray. Grill, uncovered, 4 minutes or until tender, turning once. Cut into 1-inch pieces; set aside.

3. Melt butter in large saucepan over medium heat. Add onion; cook and stir 5 minutes or until tender. Stir in flour, salt, thyme and white pepper; cook and stir 1 minute.

4. Stir beer and milk into flour mixture. Bring to a boil. Reduce heat to medium-low; simmer 1 minute. Stir in corn, potato, zucchini and cheese. Simmer, stirring constantly, until heated through.

IRISH BEEF STEW
MAKES 6 SERVINGS

2½ tablespoons vegetable oil, divided

2 pounds boneless beef chuck roast, cut into 1-inch pieces

1½ teaspoons salt, divided

¾ teaspoon black pepper, divided

1 medium onion, chopped

3 medium carrots, cut into 1-inch pieces

3 medium parsnips, cut into 1-inch pieces

1 package (8 to 10 ounces) cremini mushrooms, quartered

2 cloves garlic, minced

1 teaspoon dried thyme

1 teaspoon dried rosemary

2 bay leaves

1 can (about 15 ounces) Guinness stout

1 can (about 14 ounces) beef broth

1 tablespoon Dijon mustard

1 tablespoon tomato paste

1 tablespoon Worcestershire sauce

1 pound small yellow potatoes (about 1¼ inches), halved

1 cup frozen pearl onions

2 teaspoons water

2 teaspoons cornstarch

Chopped fresh parsley (optional)

1 Heat 2 tablespoons oil in Dutch oven or large saucepan over medium-high heat. Season beef with 1 teaspoon salt and ½ teaspoon pepper. Cook beef in two batches 5 minutes or until browned. Remove to plate.

2 Add remaining ½ tablespoon oil and chopped onion to Dutch oven; cook and stir 3 minutes or until softened. Add carrots, parsnips and mushrooms; cook 8 minutes or until vegetables soften and mushrooms release their liquid, stirring

occasionally. Add garlic, thyme, rosemary, bay leaves, remaining ½ teaspoon salt and ¼ teaspoon pepper; cook and stir 2 minutes. Add Guinness, broth, mustard, tomato paste and Worcestershire sauce; bring to a boil, scraping up any browned bits from bottom of pot. Return beef and any accumulated juices to Dutch oven; mix well.

3 Reduce heat to low; cover and cook 1 hour and 30 minutes. Stir in potatoes; cover and cook 30 minutes. Stir in pearl onions; cook, uncovered, 30 minutes or until beef and potatoes are fork-tender.

4 Stir water into cornstarch in small bowl until smooth. Add to stew; cook and stir over medium heat 3 minutes or until thickened. Garnish with parsley.

KIELBASA & CABBAGE SOUP
MAKES 8 SERVINGS

1 pound Polish kielbasa, cut into ½-inch cubes

1 package (16 ounces) coleslaw mix (shredded green cabbage and carrots)

3 cans (14½ ounces each) beef broth

1 can (12 ounces) beer or nonalcoholic malt beverage

1 cup water

½ teaspoon caraway seeds

2 cups FRENCH'S® French Fried Onions, divided

Fresh dill sprigs (optional)

1 Coat 5-quart pot or Dutch oven with nonstick cooking spray. Cook kielbasa over medium-high heat about 5 minutes or until browned. Add coleslaw mix; sauté until tender.

2 Add broth, beer, water, caraway seeds and *1 cup* French Fried Onions; bring to a boil over medium-high heat. Reduce heat to low. Simmer, uncovered, 10 minutes to blend flavors. Spoon soup into serving bowls; top with remaining onions. Garnish with fresh dill sprigs, if desired.

BEEF STEW

MAKES 8 SERVINGS

2 tablespoons olive or vegetable oil

3 pounds boneless beef chuck roast, trimmed and cut into 2-inch pieces

2 teaspoons salt

½ teaspoon black pepper

3 medium sweet or yellow onions, halved and sliced

6 medium carrots, cut into ½-inch pieces

8 ounces sliced mushrooms

¼ pound smoked ham, cut into ¼-inch pieces

2 tablespoons minced garlic

1 can (about 15 ounces) stout

1 can (about 14 ounces) beef broth

1 teaspoon sugar

1 teaspoon herbes de Provence or dried thyme

1 teaspoon Worcestershire sauce

⅓ cup cold water

2 tablespoons cornstarch

3 tablespoons chopped fresh parsley

Hot cooked wide egg noodles or steamed red potatoes (optional)

1 Heat oil in Dutch oven over medium-high heat. Add half of beef; sprinkle with salt and pepper. Cook 8 minutes or until browned on all sides. Remove to bowl; repeat with remaining beef.

2 Add onions; cook and stir over medium heat about 10 minutes. Stir in carrots, mushrooms, ham and garlic; cook and stir 10 minutes or until vegetables are softened, scraping up any browned bits from bottom of Dutch oven.

3 Return beef to Dutch oven and pour in stout and broth. (Liquid should just cover beef and vegetables; add water if needed.) Stir in sugar, herbes de Provence

and Worcestershire sauce; bring to a boil.
Reduce heat to low; cover and simmer
2 hours or until beef is fork-tender.

4 Skim fat. Stir ⅓ cup water into cornstarch
in small bowl until smooth. Stir into stew;
simmer 5 minutes. Stir in parsley. Serve over
noodles, if desired.

DINNERTIME FAVORITES

NOT YOUR MOMMA'S MEAT LOAF

MAKES 6 SERVINGS

- 2 pounds ground beef, pork and veal meat loaf mix
- ⅔ cup plain dry bread crumbs
- ½ cup finely chopped onion
- ½ cup pale ale
- ⅓ cup plus 3 tablespoons ketchup, divided
- 2 eggs
- 1 tablespoon Dijon mustard
- 2 teaspoons dried basil
- 1 teaspoon garlic powder
- 1 teaspoon salt
- ½ teaspoon black pepper

1 Preheat oven to 350°F. Spray jelly-roll pan with nonstick cooking spray.

2 Combine meat loaf mix, bread crumbs, onion, ale, 3 tablespoons ketchup, eggs, mustard, basil, garlic powder, salt and pepper in large bowl; mix well. Transfer mixture to prepared pan; shape into 10×5×2-inch loaf. Spread remaining ⅓ cup ketchup over top.

3 Bake 60 to 65 minutes or until cooked through (160°F). Let stand 10 minutes before slicing.

BEER-BRINED CHICKEN

MAKES 4 SERVINGS

- 4 cups water
- 3 cups stout or dark beer
- 2 cups apple juice
- ½ cup plus ½ teaspoon kosher salt, divided
- ½ cup packed light brown sugar
- 1 teaspoon paprika
- 1 sprig plus 1 tablespoon chopped fresh rosemary, divided
- 1 bay leaf
- 1 whole chicken (3½ to 4 pounds)
- ¼ cup (½ stick) butter, melted
- ¼ teaspoon black pepper

1 Combine water, stout, apple juice, ½ cup salt, brown sugar, paprika, rosemary sprig and bay leaf in large Dutch oven. Stir until salt and sugar are dissolved. Add chicken; cover. Refrigerate 2 to 4 hours.

2 Preheat oven to 425°F. Remove chicken from brine; pat dry. Tie drumsticks together to maintain best shape. Place on rack in roasting pan. Cover loosely with foil; bake 45 minutes.

3 Remove foil. Combine butter, 1 tablespoon chopped rosemary, remaining ½ teaspoon salt and pepper in small bowl; brush all over chicken. Bake 15 to 20 minutes or until cooked through. Remove chicken to large cutting board. Cover loosely with foil; let stand 10 minutes before cutting into pieces.

SCALLOP STIR-FRY WITH BLACK BEAN AND STOUT SAUCE

MAKES 4 TO 6 SERVINGS

- 1 can (about 15 ounces) black beans, rinsed and drained
- ⅓ cup stout
- 2 tablespoons low-sodium soy sauce
- 2 tablespoons honey
- 2 teaspoons hoisin sauce
- 2 cloves garlic, minced
- ½ teaspoon salt
- ⅛ teaspoon red pepper flakes
- 2 tablespoons olive oil
- 1 red bell pepper, cut into thin strips
- 1½ cups fresh snow peas
- 1½ cups thinly sliced carrots
- 1½ pounds sea scallops

1 Combine beans, stout, soy sauce, honey, hoisin sauce, garlic, salt and red pepper flakes in blender or food processor; process until smooth.

2 Heat oil in large skillet over medium-high heat. Add bell pepper, snow peas and carrots; stir-fry 3 minutes. Add scallops and black bean sauce; stir-fry 6 minutes or until scallops are opaque and mixture is heated through.

HAM WITH DARK BEER GRAVY
MAKES 10 TO 12 SERVINGS

1 fully cooked bone-in ham
(about 6 pounds)

1 tablespoon Dijon mustard

2 cans (6 ounces each) pineapple juice

1 bottle (12 ounces) dark beer, such as
porter

Dark Beer Gravy (recipe follows)

1 Line large roasting pan with foil.

2 Remove skin and excess fat from ham.
Score ham in diamond pattern.

3 Place ham in prepared pan. Spread mustard
over ham. Pour pineapple juice and beer
over ham. Cover and refrigerate 8 hours.

4 Preheat oven to 350°F. Cook ham 1½ hours
or until 140°F, basting every 30 minutes.
Remove ham to large cutting board. Cover
loosely with foil; let stand 15 minutes before
slicing.

5 Meanwhile, pour drippings from pan into
4-cup measuring cup. Let stand 5 minutes;
skim off and discard fat. Prepare Dark Beer
Gravy; serve with ham.

DARK BEER GRAVY
MAKES 2½ CUPS

¼ cup (½ stick) butter

¼ cup all-purpose flour

½ cup dark beer, such as porter

2 cups drippings from roasting pan

Salt and black pepper

Melt butter in small saucepan over medium
heat. Whisk in flour until blended. Cook 1 to
2 minutes, whisking constantly. Add beer to
drippings; whisk into flour mixture. Cook until
mixture is thickened and bubbly, whisking
constantly. Season with salt and pepper.

RACK OF LAMB

MAKES 4 SERVINGS

- ½ **cup Irish stout**
- 2 **tablespoons Dijon mustard**
- 2 **tablespoons chopped fresh parsley**
- 2 **tablespoons chopped fresh thyme**
- 1 **French cut rack of lamb (8 ribs, 1½ pounds)**
- ½ **teaspoon kosher salt**
- ½ **teaspoon black pepper**

1 Position rack in center of oven. Preheat oven to 400°F. Spray broiler pan and rack with nonstick cooking spray.

2 Combine stout, mustard, parsley and thyme in small bowl. Sprinkle both sides of lamb with salt and pepper; spread with stout mixture. Place lamb, bone side down, on prepared broiler pan.

3 Roast 45 minutes for medium rare (145°F) or to desired doneness. Cover with foil; let stand 10 minutes before slicing. Cut into eight pieces.

TIP

To help prevent too much browning on the tips of the bones, cover them with foil.

MUSSELS IN BEER WITH AIOLI AND TOASTS

MAKES 4 SERVINGS

1 loaf (1 pound) French bread, cut into ¼-inch slices

MUSSELS

4 pounds mussels
1 tablespoon olive oil
1 shallot, chopped
1 bottle (12 ounces) lager beer
¾ cup water

AIOLI

½ cup mayonnaise
2 cloves garlic, minced
2 tablespoons olive oil
2 teaspoons lemon juice
½ teaspoon Dijon mustard
⅛ teaspoon ground red pepper

1 Preheat oven to 450°F. Toast bread on baking sheet 15 minutes or until golden, turning once.

2 Clean mussels under cold running water. Scrape off beard from shell. Discard open mussels that will not close if tapped with knife.

3 Heat oil in large saucepan over medium heat. Add shallot; cook 1 minute or until translucent. Add lager and water. Increase heat to high; bring to a boil. Carefully add mussels. Cover; cook 3 to 5 minutes or until mussels open. Remove from heat. (Discard any mussels that do not open.)

4 Meanwhile, prepare Aioli. Combine mayonnaise, garlic, oil, lemon juice, mustard and red pepper in small bowl; mix well.

5 Spread each toast with 1 teaspoon Aioli. Serve mussels and broth with toasts.

BEEF POT PIE WITH BEER BISCUITS

MAKES 6 SERVINGS

4 slices bacon, coarsely chopped

2½ pounds beef chuck roast, cut into
1-inch pieces

2¼ teaspoons salt, divided

½ teaspoon black pepper

1 large onion, chopped

3 carrots, cut into ½-inch rounds

3 celery stalks, cut into ½-inch pieces

2 cloves garlic, minced

2⅓ cups plus 1 tablespoon all-purpose
flour, divided

1 can (about 14 ounces) reduced-sodium
beef broth

2 tablespoons Worcestershire sauce

1 teaspoon dried thyme

2½ teaspoons baking powder

6 tablespoons (¾ stick) butter, cut into
½-inch cubes

¾ cup lager

1 Preheat oven to 350°F. Cook bacon in
Dutch oven over medium heat until crisp
and browned. Remove to paper towel-lined
plate. Drain all but 2 tablespoons drippings.

2 Season beef with 1½ teaspoons salt and
pepper; add to Dutch oven in batches.
Cook and stir over medium-high heat
5 minutes or until browned. Remove to
plate with slotted spoon; reserve fat in
Dutch oven.

3 Add onion, carrots, celery and garlic to
Dutch oven; cook and stir over medium
heat 5 minutes or until vegetables are
tender. Sprinkle with ⅓ cup plus
1 tablespoon flour; stir until blended. Stir
in bacon, beef, broth, Worcestershire sauce
and thyme; bring to a boil.

4 Cover and bake 1½ hours or until beef is almost tender.

5 Meanwhile, for biscuits, whisk remaining 2 cups flour, baking powder and remaining ¾ teaspoon salt in medium bowl. Cut in butter with pastry blender or two knives until mixture resembles coarse crumbs. Stir in enough lager to make soft dough. Turn dough out onto lightly floured surface. Roll dough into 9×6-inch rectangle about ½ inch thick. Cut into six 3-inch square biscuits.

6 Remove Dutch oven from oven. *Increase oven temperature to 400°F.* Arrange biscuits over stew, overlapping if necessary. Bake 20 minutes or until biscuits are light golden brown.

BEER DOUGH PEPPERONI PIZZA

MAKES 2 (10-INCH) PIZZAS

- 1 cup lager or pale ale, at room temperature
- 3 tablespoons olive oil
- 1 package (¼ ounce) instant yeast
- 2¾ cups bread flour, plus additional for rolling dough
- 1 teaspoon salt
- 1 cup prepared pizza sauce
- 6 ounces (about 32 to 36) pepperoni slices
- 2 cups (8 ounces) shredded mozzarella cheese
- ¼ cup freshly grated Parmesan cheese

1 Combine lager, oil and yeast in medium bowl. Stir in 1 cup flour and salt. Gradually stir in enough flour to make thick dough. Turn out onto floured work surface. Knead 8 minutes or until smooth, adding flour as necessary to prevent sticking.

2 Shape dough into a ball. Place in lightly oiled medium bowl, turning to coat. Cover with plastic wrap and let rise in warm place about 1 hour or until doubled in size.

3 Preheat oven to 425°F.

4 Divide dough in half. Shape into 2 balls and place on lightly floured work surface; cover with plastic wrap. Let stand 10 minutes. Roll out each ball into 10-inch round. Remove dough rounds to ungreased baking sheets. Spread each with ½ cup pizza sauce, leaving ½-inch border around edges. Top with half of pepperoni, 1 cup mozzarella and 2 tablespoons Parmesan cheese. Repeat with remaining ingredients.

5 Bake 15 minutes or until crust is golden brown and cheese is bubbly. Let stand 3 minutes before serving.

HEAVY-DUTY MIXER

To make dough in a heavy-duty mixer, combine beer, oil and yeast in large mixer bowl. Add 1 cup flour and salt; mix on low speed with paddle blade, adding enough flour to make soft dough that cleans the bowl. Change to dough hook and knead on medium-low speed, adding more flour if needed, 8 minutes or until dough is soft, smooth and elastic.

CRISPY CHICKEN NUGGETS WITH PEANUT DIPPING SAUCE

MAKES 6 SERVINGS

DIPPING SAUCE

½ cup creamy peanut butter

½ cup coconut milk

½ cup beer

⅓ cup packed light brown sugar

3 tablespoons hoisin sauce

1 tablespoon rice vinegar

NUGGETS

¾ cup all-purpose flour

¾ teaspoon baking soda

¾ teaspoon salt

¾ cup beer

Canola oil

1½ pounds boneless skinless chicken breasts, cut into 1-inch cubes

1 For dipping sauce, whisk peanut butter, coconut milk, ½ cup beer, brown sugar, hoisin sauce and vinegar in medium saucepan. Bring to a simmer over medium heat; cook and stir 3 minutes or until thickened. Transfer to serving bowl.

2 For nuggets, combine flour, baking soda and salt in medium bowl. Stir in ¾ cup beer until smooth.

3 Heat 2 inches oil in Dutch oven over medium heat to 360°F. Line large baking sheet with paper towels. Add 12 chicken pieces to beer mixture, stirring to coat. Shake off excess batter and carefully add to hot oil. Cook 3 minutes or until golden and puffed and chicken is cooked through. Remove to prepared baking sheet. Repeat with remaining batter and chicken. Serve with dipping sauce.

PASTRAMI REUBEN SANDWICHES WITH BEER KRAUT

MAKES 4 SERVINGS

1 tablespoon canola oil

½ cup thinly sliced Vidalia or other sweet onion

1 cup well-drained sauerkraut

1 teaspoon sugar

½ cup beer

Unsalted butter, softened

8 slices rye bread

½ cup Russian dressing

4 slices Swiss cheese

1 pound thinly sliced pastrami

1 Heat oil in medium skillet over medium-high heat. Add onion; cook and stir 2 minutes or until slightly softened. Add sauerkraut and sugar; cook 3 minutes. Pour in beer; cook 3 minutes or until evaporated, stirring occasionally. Remove from heat.

2 Butter one side of bread slices. Place 4 slices bread, butter side down, on work surface. Spread with 1 tablespoon Russian dressing. Top with one fourth of sauerkraut mixture, 1 slice cheese and one fourth of pastrami. Spread unbuttered sides of remaining 4 slices bread with remaining Russian dressing; place butter side up on pastrami.

3 Heat large nonstick skillet over medium heat. Place two sandwiches in skillet; press firmly with spatula. Cook 3 minutes or until bread is golden. Turn; place second large skillet on top of sandwiches and press firmly. Cook 4 minutes or until golden. Repeat with remaining two sandwiches.

PULLED PORK QUESADILLAS
MAKES 8 SERVINGS

1 pound pork tenderloin, cut into 3-inch pieces

1 cup beer

1 cup barbecue sauce

1 teaspoon chili powder

4 (8-inch) flour tortillas

2⅔ cups shredded Monterey Jack cheese

Optional toppings: salsa, sour cream and chopped fresh cilantro

1 Combine pork, beer, barbecue sauce and chili powder in large saucepan over medium-high heat; bring to a boil. Reduce heat to medium-low. Cover; simmer 50 minutes or until pork is tender, stirring occasionally. Remove pork to large bowl; shred using two forks.

2 Bring sauce to a boil over medium-high heat; boil 8 to 10 minutes or until thickened. Add ¾ cup sauce to shredded pork; discard remaining sauce.

3 Place tortillas on work surface. Layer bottom half of each tortilla evenly with pork and cheese. Fold top halves of tortillas over filling to form semicircle.

4 Heat large nonstick skillet over medium heat. Add two quesadillas; cook 6 to 8 minutes or until golden and cheese is melted, turning once. Transfer to cutting board. Cut into six wedges. Repeat with remaining quesadillas. Top as desired.

PUB-STYLE FISH & CHIPS
MAKES 4 SERVINGS

¾ cup all-purpose flour, plus additional for dusting fish

½ cup flat beer

Vegetable oil for frying

3 large or 4 medium russet potatoes

1 egg, separated

Salt

1 pound cod fillets

Prepared tartar sauce

Lemon wedges

1 Combine ¾ cup flour, beer and 2 teaspoons oil in small bowl; mix well. Cover; refrigerate 30 minutes to 2 hours.

2 Peel potatoes and cut into ¾-inch sticks. Place in large bowl of cold water. Pour at least 2 inches of oil into deep heavy saucepan or deep fryer; heat over medium heat to 320°F. Drain and thoroughly dry potatoes. Fry in batches 3 minutes or until slightly softened but not browned. Drain on paper towel-lined plate.

3 Stir egg yolk into cold flour mixture. Beat egg white in medium bowl with electric mixer at medium-high speed until soft peaks form. Fold egg white into flour mixture. Season batter with pinch of salt.

4 Preheat oven to 200°F. Heat 2 inches oil in large saucepan to 365°F. Cut fish into pieces about 6 inches long and 2 to 3 inches wide; remove any pin bones. Dust fish with flour; dip fish into batter, shaking off excess. Lower carefully into oil; cook in batches 4 to 6 minutes or until batter is browned and fish is cooked through, turning once. Do not crowd saucepan. (Allow temperature of oil to return to 365°F between batches.) Drain on paper towel-lined plate; keep warm in oven.

5 Return potatoes to hot oil; cook in batches 5 minutes or until browned and crisp. Drain on paper towel-lined plate; sprinkle with salt. Serve fish with potatoes, tartar sauce and lemon wedges.

ROASTED GARLIC & STOUT MAC & CHEESE

MAKES 8 TO 10 SERVINGS

- 1 head garlic
- 1 tablespoon olive oil
- 6 tablespoons (¾ stick) butter, divided, plus additional for pan
- 1¼ teaspoons salt, divided
- 1 cup panko bread crumbs
- ¼ cup all-purpose flour
- ½ teaspoon black pepper
- 2 cups whole milk
- ¾ cup Irish stout
- 2 cups (8 ounces) shredded sharp Cheddar cheese
- 2 cups (8 ounces) shredded Dubliner cheese
- 1 pound cellentani pasta,* cooked and drained

Or substitute elbow macaroni, penne or other favorite pasta shape.

1 Preheat oven to 375°F. Butter 4-quart shallow baking dish.

2 Place garlic on 10-inch piece of foil; drizzle with oil and crimp shut. Place on small baking sheet; bake 30 minutes or until tender. Cool 15 minutes; squeeze cloves into small bowl. Mash into smooth paste.

3 Microwave 2 tablespoons butter in medium bowl until melted. Stir in ¼ teaspoon salt until dissolved. Stir in panko until well blended.

4 Melt remaining 4 tablespoons butter in large saucepan over medium heat. Add flour; cook and stir until lightly browned. Stir in roasted garlic paste, remaining 1 teaspoon salt and pepper. Slowly whisk in milk and stout. Simmer until thickened, whisking constantly. Remove from heat;

whisk in cheeses, ½ cup at a time, until melted. Combine cheese mixture and pasta in large bowl. Spoon into prepared baking dish; sprinkle with panko mixture.

5 Bake 40 minutes or until bubbly and topping is golden brown. Let stand 10 minutes before serving.

JALAPEÑO BEANS

MAKES 4 TO 6 SERVINGS

- 1 tablespoon vegetable oil
- 1 small onion, finely chopped
- 1 teaspoon ground cumin
- 1 teaspoon garlic powder
- ½ teaspoon smoked paprika
- ¼ teaspoon ground red pepper
- 3 tablespoons chopped pickled jalapeño peppers
- 2 cans (about 15 ounces each) chili beans (made with pinto beans)
- ⅓ cup dark lager beer
- 1 tablespoon white vinegar
- 1 teaspoon sugar
- ½ teaspoon hot pepper sauce
- Salt and black pepper

1 Heat oil in medium saucepan over medium-high heat. Add onion; cook and stir 2 minutes or until translucent. Add cumin, garlic powder, paprika and red pepper; cook and stir 1 minute. Add pickled jalapeños; cook and stir 30 seconds.

2 Stir in beans, beer, vinegar, sugar and hot pepper sauce; bring to a boil. Reduce heat to medium-low; cook 15 minutes, stirring occasionally. Season with salt and black pepper. Beans will thicken upon standing.

CHEDDAR-BEER HUSH PUPPIES

MAKES ABOUT 36 HUSH PUPPIES

Vegetable oil for frying

1½ cups medium grain cornmeal

1 cup all-purpose flour

2 tablespoons sugar

1 teaspoon baking powder

1 teaspoon baking soda

1 teaspoon salt

¼ teaspoon black pepper

1 bottle (12 ounces) lager beer

1 egg, beaten

¾ cup (3 ounces) shredded Cheddar cheese

2 jalapeño peppers, seeded and minced

1 Fill large saucepan with 3 inches of oil and heat to 350°F. Line baking sheet with three layers of paper towels.

2 Whisk together cornmeal, flour, sugar, baking powder, baking soda, salt and black pepper in large bowl. Whisk together beer and egg until combined in separate medium bowl. Gradually whisk beer mixture into cornmeal mixture until smooth. Stir in cheese and jalapeño peppers.

3 Working in batches, drop heaping tablespoonfuls of batter into oil. Fry 2 minutes or until golden brown, turning occasionally. Transfer to prepared baking sheet to drain. Repeat with remaining batter. Serve immediately.

BAKING WITH BEER

SPICED PUMPKIN BEER BREAD
MAKES 12 SERVINGS

2¼ cups all-purpose flour

2 teaspoons baking powder

1 teaspoon ground cinnamon

¾ teaspoon baking soda

½ teaspoon salt

¼ teaspoon ground nutmeg

⅛ teaspoon ground cloves

1½ cups sugar

1¼ cups canned pumpkin

¾ cup lager

½ cup canola oil

2 eggs

½ cup walnuts, coarsely chopped

1 Preheat oven to 350°F. Grease and flour 9×5-inch loaf pan.

2 Combine flour, baking powder, cinnamon, baking soda, salt, nutmeg and cloves in large bowl; mix well. Combine sugar, pumpkin, lager, oil and eggs in medium bowl; beat until well blended. Add to flour mixture; stir just until dry ingredients are moistened. Stir in walnuts. Pour batter into prepared pan.

3 Bake 65 minutes or until toothpick inserted into center comes out clean. Cool in pan 10 minutes; remove to wire rack. Cool 1 hour before serving.

GINGERBREAD WITH LEMON SAUCE

MAKES 9 SERVINGS

- 2½ cups all-purpose flour
- 1½ teaspoons ground cinnamon
- 1 teaspoon ground ginger
- ½ teaspoon baking soda
- ½ teaspoon salt
- ½ cup (1 stick) butter, softened
- ¾ cup packed brown sugar
- ⅓ cup light molasses
- 1 egg
- ¾ cup stout, at room temperature
- Lemon Sauce (recipe follows)
- Grated lemon peel (optional)

1 Preheat oven to 350°F. Spray bottom of 9-inch square baking pan with nonstick cooking spray. Combine flour, cinnamon, ginger, baking soda and salt in medium bowl.

2 Beat butter and brown sugar in large bowl with electric mixer on medium speed until light and fluffy. Add molasses and egg; beat until blended. Add flour mixture alternately with stout, beating until blended after each addition. Pour batter evenly into prepared pan.

3 Bake 35 to 40 minutes or until toothpick inserted into center comes out clean. Cool completely in pan on wire rack. Prepare Lemon Sauce.

4 Serve cake with sauce; sprinkle with lemon peel, if desired.

LEMON SAUCE

- 1 **cup granulated sugar**
- ¾ **cup whipping cream**
- ½ **cup (1 stick) butter**
- 1 **tablespoon lemon juice**
- 2 **teaspoons grated lemon peel**

Combine granulated sugar, cream and butter in small saucepan; cook and stir over medium heat until butter is melted. Reduce heat to low; simmer 5 minutes. Stir in lemon juice and lemon peel. Cool slightly.

BEER PRETZELS

MAKES 12 PRETZELS

¼ cup warm water

1 package (¼ ounce) active dry yeast

1 tablespoon sugar

1 tablespoon olive oil

1 teaspoon kosher salt, divided

1 cup brown ale, at room temperature

3¾ to 4 cups all-purpose flour

2 cups hot water

1 teaspoon baking soda

1 egg, well beaten

2 tablespoons butter, melted

Mustard (optional)

1 Place warm water in large bowl; sprinkle with yeast. Let stand 5 minutes or until mixture is bubbly. Add sugar, oil, ¾ teaspoon salt, ale and 3¾ cups flour; stir to form soft dough. Knead on floured surface 6 to 8 minutes or until smooth and elastic, adding additional flour by tablespoonfuls if necessary.

2 Place dough in greased medium bowl; turn to grease top. Cover and let rise in warm place 45 minutes or until doubled in size.

3 Punch down dough. Divide into 12 pieces. Roll each piece into a rope about 20 inches long. If dough becomes too difficult to roll, let stand 10 minutes. Shape ropes into pretzels.

4 Preheat oven to 425°F. Line baking sheet with parchment paper or spray with nonstick cooking spray. Stir hot water into baking soda in pie plate until blended. Dip pretzels into mixture; place on prepared baking sheet. Cover loosely and let stand in warm place 15 to 20 minutes. Brush pretzels with egg; sprinkle with remaining ¼ teaspoon salt.

5 Bake 10 minutes or until golden brown. Brush pretzels with melted butter. Serve with mustard, if desired.

VARIATION

Sprinkle a small amount of shredded cheese over pretzels before baking—Parmesan, Asiago or Cheddar. Or add ½ cup (2 ounces) shredded Cheddar cheese to batter when you are almost finished kneading in step 1.

CHERRY SCONES
MAKES 8 SCONES

- 1½ cups all-purpose flour
- 1 cup whole wheat flour
- 3 tablespoons granulated sugar
- 2 teaspoons baking powder
- ¼ teaspoon salt
- ½ cup butter-flavored shortening
- ½ cup honey beer
- ⅓ cup milk
- 1 egg, beaten
- ¾ cup dried cherries
- 1 teaspoon raw sugar
- Fresh fruit and cherry preserves (optional)

1 Preheat oven to 425°F. Combine flours, granulated sugar, baking powder and salt in large bowl. Cut in shortening with pastry blender or two knives until mixture resembles coarse crumbs. Combine beer, milk and egg in medium bowl; stir into flour mixture. Stir in cherries. Knead gently on floured surface four times.

2 Shape dough into a ball and place on ungreased baking sheet. Pat into 8-inch circle. Score dough into eight wedges (do not separate). Sprinkle with raw sugar. Bake 18 minutes or until golden brown. Cut into wedges. Serve with fruit and preserves, if desired.

CHOCOLATE STOUT CAKE
MAKES 12 SERVINGS

- 2 cups all-purpose flour
- ¾ cup unsweetened cocoa powder
- 1 teaspoon baking soda
- ¼ teaspoon salt
- 1 cup packed brown sugar
- ¾ cup (1½ sticks) butter, softened
- ½ cup granulated sugar
- 1 teaspoon vanilla
- 3 eggs
- 1 cup stout, at room temperature
- Cream Cheese Frosting
  (recipe follows)

1 Preheat oven to 350°F. Spray 13×9-inch baking pan with nonstick cooking spray. Combine flour, cocoa, baking soda and salt in medium bowl.

2 Beat brown sugar, butter and granulated sugar in large bowl with electric mixer at medium speed until light and fluffy. Beat in vanilla. Add eggs, one at a time, beating well after each addition. Add flour mixture alternately with stout, beating until blended after each addition. Pour batter evenly into prepared pan.

3 Bake 35 to 40 minutes or until toothpick inserted into center comes out clean. Cool on wire rack.

4 Prepare Cream Cheese Frosting. Spread frosting over cake.

CREAM CHEESE FROSTING
MAKES 2½ CUPS

1 package (8 ounces) cream cheese, softened

¼ cup (½ stick) butter, softened

4 cups powdered sugar

1 teaspoon vanilla

1 to 2 tablespoons milk

Beat cream cheese and butter in large bowl with electric mixer at medium speed until creamy. Gradually beat in powdered sugar and vanilla until smooth. Add enough milk to make spreadable frosting; beat until smooth.

PEPPERONI CHEESE BREAD
MAKES 2 (12-INCH) LOAVES

Oregano-Infused Dipping Oil
  (recipe follows)
1 package (¼ ounce) active dry yeast
1 cup warm beer
½ cup warm milk
2¼ cups all-purpose flour, divided
1 cup rye flour
1 tablespoon dried basil
1 teaspoon sugar
1 teaspoon salt
1 teaspoon red pepper flakes
1 cup (4 ounces) shredded sharp
  Cheddar cheese
1 cup finely chopped pepperoni
1 tablespoon olive oil

1 Prepare Oregano-Infused Dipping Oil.

2 In large mixing bowl, dissolve yeast in warm beer and milk. Stir in 2 cups all-purpose flour, rye flour, basil, sugar, salt and red pepper flakes until smooth. Stir in enough remaining all-purpose flour to form stiff dough. Turn onto a well-floured surface; sprinkle with cheese and pepperoni. Knead 5 to 6 minutes or until smooth and elastic. Transfer to greased bowl; turning once to grease top. Cover and let rise about 1 hour in warm place until doubled in size.

3 Punch dough down; divide in half. Shape into two 12-inch loaves. Place on greased baking sheets. Cover; let rise in warm place 45 minutes or until doubled again. Preheat oven to 350°F. Bake bread 30 to 35 minutes or until golden brown. Serve with Oregano-Infused Dipping Oil.

OREGANO-INFUSED DIPPING OIL

Combine 2 tablespoons olive oil,
½ teaspoon black pepper, 1 tablespoon
chopped green olives and 1 sprig fresh
oregano. Let sit several hours before
serving to blend flavors.

MUSTARD BEER BISCUITS
MAKES ABOUT 1 DOZEN

- 2 cups all-purpose flour
- 2 teaspoons baking powder
- ¾ teaspoon salt
- ¼ cup shortening
- ¼ cup (½ stick) butter
- ½ cup beer
- 1 tablespoon plus 1 teaspoon yellow mustard, divided
- 1 tablespoon milk

1 Preheat oven to 425°F. Grease large baking sheet. Combine flour, baking powder and salt in large bowl. Cut in shortening and butter with pastry blender or two knives until mixture resembles coarse crumbs. Combine beer and 1 tablespoon mustard in small bowl. Add beer mixture to flour mixture; stir just until moistened. Knead gently on floured surface eight times.

2 Pat dough to ½-inch thickness. Cut out biscuits with 2-inch round cutter. Reroll scraps and cut out additional biscuits. Place 1 inch apart on prepared baking sheet. Combine remaining 1 teaspoon mustard with milk in small bowl. Brush over tops of biscuits. Bake 13 minutes or until lightly browned.

BOSTON BROWN BREAD MUFFINS
MAKES 12 MUFFINS

- ½ cup rye flour
- ½ cup whole wheat flour
- ½ cup yellow cornmeal
- 1½ teaspoons baking soda
- ¾ teaspoon salt
- 1 cup buttermilk
- ⅓ cup packed dark brown sugar
- ⅓ cup molasses
- ⅓ cup dark beer
- 1 egg
- 1 cup golden raisins
- Cream cheese, softened

1 Preheat oven to 400°F. Grease 12 standard (2½-inch) muffin cups or line with paper baking cups.

2 Combine flours, cornmeal, baking soda and salt in large bowl. Combine buttermilk, brown sugar, molasses, beer and egg in medium bowl. Add to flour mixture along with raisins; stir until combined. Spoon batter into prepared muffin cups, filling three-fourths full.

3 Bake 15 minutes or until toothpick inserted into centers comes out clean. Serve with cream cheese.

GINGER STOUT CAKE
MAKES 12 TO 15 SERVINGS

- 2 cups all-purpose flour
- 2 teaspoons ground ginger
- 1½ teaspoons baking powder
- 1½ teaspoons baking soda
- ¾ teaspoon ground cinnamon, plus additional for garnish
- ½ teaspoon salt
- ¼ teaspoon ground cloves
- ½ cup (1 stick) butter, softened
- 1 tablespoon grated fresh ginger *or* 1 teaspoon ground ginger
- 1 cup granulated sugar
- ½ cup packed brown sugar
- 3 eggs
- 1 bottle (11 ounces) Irish stout
- ½ cup molasses
- Whipped cream (optional)

1 Preheat oven to 350°F. Grease 13×9-inch baking pan. Combine flour, ground ginger, baking powder, baking soda, ¾ teaspoon cinnamon, salt and cloves in medium bowl.

2 Beat butter and grated ginger in large bowl with electric mixer at medium speed until creamy. Add granulated sugar and brown sugar; beat until light and fluffy. Add eggs, one at a time, beating well after each addition.

3 Combine stout and molasses in medium bowl; mix well. Alternately add flour mixture and stout mixture to butter mixture, beating well after each addition. Pour batter into prepared pan.

4 Bake 45 minutes or until toothpick inserted into center comes out clean. Cool completely in pan on wire rack. Garnish with whipped cream and additional cinnamon.

BEER, CARAMELIZED ONION, BACON AND PARMESAN MUFFINS

MAKES 12 MUFFINS

- 6 slices bacon, chopped
- 2 cups chopped onions
- 3 teaspoons sugar, divided
- ¼ teaspoon dried thyme
- 1½ cups all-purpose flour
- ¾ cup grated Parmesan cheese
- 2 teaspoons baking powder
- ½ teaspoon salt
- ¾ cup lager or other light-colored beer
- 2 eggs
- ¼ cup extra virgin olive oil

1 Preheat oven to 375°F. Grease 12 standard (2½-inch) muffin cups.

2 Cook bacon in large skillet over medium heat until crisp, stirring occasionally. Drain on paper towel-lined plate. Add onions, 1 teaspoon sugar and thyme to skillet; cook 12 minutes or until onions are golden brown, stirring occasionally. Cool 5 minutes; stir in bacon.

3 Combine flour, cheese, baking powder, salt and remaining 2 teaspoons sugar in large bowl. Whisk lager, eggs and oil in medium bowl. Add to flour mixture; stir just until dry ingredients are moistened. Gently stir in onion mixture. Spoon batter evenly into prepared muffin cups.

4 Bake 15 minutes or until toothpick inserted into centers comes out clean. Cool in pan 5 minutes; remove to wire rack. Serve warm.

CHOCOLATE-RASPBERRY BEER BROWNIES

MAKES 16 SERVINGS

- 4 ounces unsweetened chocolate, chopped
- 10 tablespoons unsalted butter, plus additional for pan
- 1½ cups sugar
- ½ cup Belgian white ale, at room temperature
- 3 eggs
- 2 teaspoons vanilla extract
- 1 cup all-purpose flour, plus additional for pan
- ½ teaspoon baking powder
- ¼ teaspoon salt
- ½ cup seedless raspberry jam, stirred until smooth

1 Preheat oven to 350°F. Butter and flour 9-inch square baking pan.

2 Combine chocolate and 10 tablespoons butter in small saucepan over low heat; cook and stir until melted. Remove to large bowl; cool 5 minutes. Whisk sugar, ale, eggs and vanilla in medium bowl. Combine 1 cup flour, baking powder and salt in another medium bowl.

3 Stir ale mixture into chocolate mixture; blend well. Fold in flour mixture just until moistened. Pour batter into prepared baking pan. Drizzle raspberry jam over batter.

4 Bake 30 to 35 minutes or until toothpick inserted into center comes out with moist crumbs attached. Cool completely in pan on wire rack. Cut into bars.

GINGERBREAD STOUT CUPCAKES WITH STOUT BUTTERCREAM
MAKES 12 CUPCAKES

CUPCAKES

1¼ cups all-purpose flour

1 teaspoon ground ginger

1 teaspoon ground cinnamon

¾ teaspoon baking soda

¼ teaspoon salt

½ cup (1 stick) unsalted butter, softened

½ cup packed light brown sugar

1 egg

⅓ cup molasses (not blackstrap)

½ cup flat stout, at room temperature (open at least 1 hour before using)

STOUT BUTTERCREAM

1½ cups powdered sugar, sifted

¼ cup (½ stick) unsalted butter, softened

3 tablespoons flat stout, at room temperature, as needed

¼ cup finely chopped crystallized ginger

1 Preheat oven to 350°F. Line 12 standard (2½-inch) muffin cups with paper baking cups.

2 For cupcakes, combine flour, ground ginger, cinnamon, baking soda and salt in large bowl. Beat butter in medium bowl with electric mixer on high speed 1 minute or until smooth. Gradually beat in brown sugar 3 minutes or until light in color and texture. Beat in egg and molasses. Reduce speed to low. Add flour mixture one third at a time, alternating with stout, ending with flour mixture; mix until smooth, scraping down sides of bowl with spatula. Spoon batter into prepared muffin cups, filling two-thirds full; smooth tops.

3 Bake 20 minutes or until toothpick inserted into centers comes out clean. Cool in pan 5 minutes. Remove to wire rack; cool completely.

4 Meanwhile, for frosting, beat powdered sugar and butter together in medium bowl with electric mixer on low speed until crumbly. Gradually beat in enough stout to make spreadable frosting. Stir in crystallized ginger. Frost cupcakes and serve at room temperature.

ROSEMARY LAGER FOCACCIA
MAKES 12 SERVINGS

1¼ cups lager

4 tablespoons extra virgin olive oil, divided

1 package (¼ ounce) active dry yeast

1 tablespoon sugar

3 cups plus ¼ cup all-purpose flour, divided

2 teaspoons coarse salt, divided

¼ cup fresh rosemary leaves

1 Place lager in medium microwavable bowl. Microwave on HIGH 25 seconds. Stir in 3 tablespoons oil, yeast and sugar; let stand 5 minutes or until foamy.

2 Combine 3 cups flour and 1 teaspoon salt in large bowl. Stir in lager mixture until dough pulls away from sides of bowl. Knead dough on floured surface, adding remaining flour 1 tablespoon at a time as necessary until smooth, elastic and slightly sticky. Transfer to oiled large bowl, turning to grease top. Cover; let stand in warm place 1½ hours or until doubled in size.

3 Preheat oven to 325°F. Spray large baking sheet with nonstick cooking spray. Place dough on prepared baking sheet. Stretch into 15×10-inch rectangle. Cover; let stand 30 minutes.

4 Brush dough with remaining 1 tablespoon oil. Sprinkle with rosemary and remaining 1 teaspoon salt. Bake 30 minutes or until golden brown. Cool 10 minutes before slicing. Serve warm or at room temperature.

NOTE

To reheat, wrap leftovers in foil and warm 10 minutes in a 300°F oven before serving.

INDEX

A

INDEX

INDEX

METRIC CONVERSION CHART

VOLUME MEASUREMENTS (dry)

$^1/_8$ teaspoon = 0.5 mL
$^1/_4$ teaspoon = 1 mL
$^1/_2$ teaspoon = 2 mL
$^3/_4$ teaspoon = 4 mL
1 teaspoon = 5 mL
1 tablespoon = 15 mL
2 tablespoons = 30 mL
$^1/_4$ cup = 60 mL
$^1/_3$ cup = 75 mL
$^1/_2$ cup = 125 mL
$^2/_3$ cup = 150 mL
$^3/_4$ cup = 175 mL
1 cup = 250 mL
2 cups = 1 pint = 500 mL
3 cups = 750 mL
4 cups = 1 quart = 1 L

VOLUME MEASUREMENTS (fluid)

1 fluid ounce (2 tablespoons) = 30 mL
4 fluid ounces ($^1/_2$ cup) = 125 mL
8 fluid ounces (1 cup) = 250 mL
12 fluid ounces (1$^1/_2$ cups) = 375 mL
16 fluid ounces (2 cups) = 500 mL

WEIGHTS (mass)

$^1/_2$ ounce = 15 g
1 ounce = 30 g
3 ounces = 90 g
4 ounces = 120 g
8 ounces = 225 g
10 ounces = 285 g
12 ounces = 360 g
16 ounces = 1 pound = 450 g

DIMENSIONS

$^1/_{16}$ inch = 2 mm
$^1/_8$ inch = 3 mm
$^1/_4$ inch = 6 mm
$^1/_2$ inch = 1.5 cm
$^3/_4$ inch = 2 cm
1 inch = 2.5 cm

OVEN TEMPERATURES

250°F = 120°C
275°F = 140°C
300°F = 150°C
325°F = 160°C
350°F = 180°C
375°F = 190°C
400°F = 200°C
425°F = 220°C
450°F = 230°C

BAKING PAN SIZES

Utensil	Size in Inches/Quarts	Metric Volume	Size in Centimeters
Baking or	8×8×2	2 L	20×20×5
Cake Pan	9×9×2	2.5 L	23×23×5
(square or	12×8×2	3 L	30×20×5
rectangular)	13×9×2	3.5 L	33×23×5
Loaf Pan	8×4×3	1.5 L	20×10×7
	9×5×3	2 L	23×13×7
Round Layer	8×1½	1.2 L	20×4
Cake Pan	9×1½	1.5 L	23×4
Pie Plate	8×1¼	750 mL	20×3
	9×1¼	1 L	23×3
Baking Dish	1 quart	1 L	—
or Casserole	1½ quart	1.5 L	—
	2 quart	2 L	—